# Look, Heart…
# Listen, Soul

## Vivian Kearney

Look, Heart… Listen, Soul
©2019, Vivian Kearney
Cover illustration © 2019, Vivian Kearney
Pukiyari Publishers

The total or partial reproduction of this book is prohibited. This book cannot be totally or partially reproduced, transmitted, copied or stored using any means or ways including graphic, electronics or mechanic without the consent and written authorization of the author, except in the case of small quotes used in articles and written comments about the book.

ISBN-13: 978-1-63065-122-0

### PUKIYARI PUBLISHERS
www.pukiyari.com

Dedicated to my beloved husband Milo, our dear families and the always amazing world inside, outside and beyond.

Thanks to God, friends, mentors, spiritual guides and our daughter-in-law, Lisa Kearney for her compassionate poem and to our patient editor, Ani.

# Table of Contents

*Inside* ................................................................ *17*

    Look, Heart… Listen, Soul ............................. 19

    Autobiography ................................................. 20

    Moving On From Childhood .......................... 21

    Our Ghosts ....................................................... 22

    Aging Recollections ....................................... 23

    Location, Location .......................................... 24

    When I Die ...................................................... 25

    Shatterlands .................................................... 26

    How Did That Happen? .................................. 27

    Fatigue ............................................................. 28

    Time Conundrum ............................................ 29

    Looking For ..................................................... 30

    Nostalgia, Solestalgia ..................................... 31

    Healthy Goals ................................................. 32

    Once Advised ................................................. 33

    Third Age Meditation ..................................... 34

    Real or Fake ................................................... 35

    Illness, Loss .................................................... 36

    Best Intentions ................................................ 37

    In Our Day ....................................................... 38

| | |
|---|---|
| Nurture | 39 |
| Forgive Me | 40 |
| Reasons and Excuses | 41 |
| More Needed For Whom? | 42 |
| Twenty-Three and Everybody | 43 |
| Time-Machined | 44 |
| Avatars | 45 |
| Don't Judge | 46 |
| Listen, Mind | 47 |
| Impressions Revised | 48 |
| Wings | 49 |
| Just Wondering | 50 |
| Your Body Knows | 51 |
| Who Are You? | 52 |
| Teachable Moments | 53 |
| Evolving Zen Masters | 54 |
| Aging Staircase | 55 |
| The Supposed Healer | 56 |
| Insomnia | 57 |
| Voiced Insomnia | 58 |
| Dream Diaries | 59 |
| Room at Dawn | 60 |
| I'm So Grateful | 61 |

While I Wasn't Looking .................................................... 62
Dancing in the Light ....................................................... 63
Hidden Possibilities ....................................................... 64
Enough Room .................................................................. 65
A Cinderella House ......................................................... 66
Cleaning by Tenses ......................................................... 67
Certain Chores ................................................................ 68
My Friend, This House ................................................... 69
Inside as Outside ............................................................ 70
Who Loves Ironing? ....................................................... 71
To a Yellow Plaid Shirt .................................................. 72
*Petite Fleur* .................................................................. 73
Find Your Thanks ........................................................... 74
Out of Date ..................................................................... 75
Downsizing Pains ........................................................... 76
Typewriter Stroke ........................................................... 78
Musical – Then and Now ............................................... 79

## *Outside* ............................................................. *81*

Morning Present ............................................................. 83
The Street Hums ............................................................. 84
Sun Commission ............................................................. 85
Bee Efficient ................................................................... 86
It's Time .......................................................................... 87

| | |
|---|---|
| Taffy Time | 88 |
| Eventide | 89 |
| Great Room at the | 90 |
| Southwestern School of Art | 90 |
| Garden at Trinity University | 91 |
| On the Way to the MARC (Medical and Research Center) | 92 |
| From the Heights | 93 |
| Get-Well Bouquet | 94 |
| Transported to the Ultra-Sound Room | 95 |
| Waiting for Results | 96 |
| Unbooked Half-Room | 97 |
| Hearing What? | 98 |
| At the Dealership | 99 |
| Good Listeners | 100 |
| Lessons for a Substitute | 101 |
| Temporary | 102 |
| Before Retirement | 103 |
| After Retirement | 104 |
| Campus Life Restarted (Without Me) | 105 |
| Little Boy Cute | 106 |
| Sister Nature | 107 |
| Nature's Clothes | 108 |
| Not Helping | 109 |

| | |
|---|---|
| Drought | 110 |
| Out in the Microscopic World | 111 |
| Honor the Presents | 112 |
| Stop Objectifying | 113 |
| Cattle Moved | 114 |
| No Matter How Pretty | 115 |
| Can Anyone Hear? | 116 |
| Wonderfully Framed | 117 |
| Fish, Boats and Butterflies | 118 |
| Look Up | 119 |
| Adorable, Vestigial | 120 |
| *Quo Vadis?* – Where Are You Going? | 121 |
| Leading, Led | 122 |
| Temporary Memorial | 123 |
| Watching | 124 |
| Thin Strands | 125 |
| Limestone Keepers | 126 |
| Code Switching | 127 |
| Baroque Painting in the Sky | 128 |
| I'll Get the Mail | 129 |
| April Fool | 130 |
| Flower Music | 131 |
| Record Breaking Heat | 132 |

Atacama Desert Discovery ................................................ 133

Future Explorers .............................................................. 134

Still Summer .................................................................... 135

Cloud Personalities ......................................................... 136

Tell Me ............................................................................ 137

Finally ............................................................................. 138

The Character of Water .................................................. 139

Sleepless in the Sky ........................................................ 140

Oak Tree's Concern ........................................................ 141

Moon Moods ................................................................... 142

Moth or Butterfly? .......................................................... 143

Snow in San Antonio ...................................................... 144

Sacrifice .......................................................................... 145

Don't Give Up ................................................................ 146

Winter to Spring ............................................................. 147

Resting by the Side of I-10 to Brownsville .................... 148

Driving Back from Brownsville ..................................... 149

We're Ready ................................................................... 151

Mercado, San Antonio .................................................... 152

Walk in Schnabel Park ................................................... 153

After Movie – *One Year in Siberia* ............................... 154

After E.M. Forster .......................................................... 155

Where Do They Come From? ........................................ 156

Word Game Prizes ........................................................ 158
Bitter Flowers ............................................................. 159

# *Beyond* ................................................ *161*

Words Once Acquired ................................................ 163
To Write On ................................................................ 164
After Emily Dickinson – *To Make a Prairie* ............. 165
Library Analogy ......................................................... 166
Books Ubiquitous ....................................................... 168
Book Club with C.S. Lewis, Martin Buber ................ 169
After *Plato and a Platypus Walk Into a Bar* – by T.W.Cathcart and D.M. Klein .................................... 170
Caves – After Plato's allegory in ............................... 171
*The Republic* ............................................................ 171
After *Gravity and Grace* by Simone Weil ................ 172
After *Brontë* by Glynn Hughes ................................ 173
After NPR Interview with Michael Collins – Astronaut ................................................................................... 174
Precursor .................................................................... 175
Notre Dame, Paris, April 15, 2019 ............................ 176
Guatemala Travelogue ............................................... 177
Forever a Road Trip ................................................... 178
The Kaleidescope Cure .............................................. 179
Soular Universe ......................................................... 180

Dreams to Poems .............................................................. 181
One Difference Makes a Difference ........................... 182
Poems to Prayer ............................................................ 183
Poet Tree Island ............................................................ 184
Possibilities ................................................................... 185
Poetry Assembly Line ................................................. 186
You Are My Favorite Poem ........................................ 187
Once Told ...................................................................... 188
*Bashert* – Arranged in Heaven ................................... 189
Out of the Clear Blue Sky ........................................... 190
In the Kingdom of Love .............................................. 191
Not Even Half-Begun .................................................. 192
As One ........................................................................... 193
Towards the End .......................................................... 194
Photos with Radio ........................................................ 195
We Are All Walking Wounded ................................... 196
Sermon at St. Francis .................................................. 198
I Corinthins:13 – Beyond ............................................ 199

*Inside*

# Look, Heart… Listen, Soul

Look, heart
The plants around
Cannot grow
Without rain and sun
From above

Thus, their healthy identities
Are tied up with the heavens

Listen, soul
You cannot survive
Without supernatural love
Spiritual food
From above
To share
To steward

Thus, your eternal well-being and identity
Is tied up with God, your Creator

# Autobiography

For the story of my life
I keep mulling anew
I mostly don't realize

My perspective
Isn't the last word

Since I am
The undependable
First person narrator

## Moving On From Childhood

Past the shames and beyond the hurts
Via boats of words, rivers of time
Some thoughts rhyme, others float alone
Some pains stay, some can be abandoned
To soon veiled landscapes
Of previous lives

# Our Ghosts

Our ghosts, our near ones passed
Hang around here for several years
To see how we handle
Those earthly incongruities
And heavenly mercies

Helping us
To recollect histories
Convicting us
To resolutions remorseful

Then we move on
Their roads differ
As they enjoy their sky walks

Leaving behind
Their sayings, conversations,
Vibes and songs

## Aging Recollections

Cherished
Moments in long-term memory
Kept safe, strung in rosaries
Sparkle like polished diamonds
Though gone
Are the accompanying melodies

Why these for me
And not those remembered by others
Chosen for their collections
Tenderly

I may sometimes
Review mine cheerfully
But they're probably too far back
For much social currency

## Location, Location

Never forget the power of place,
Your geographical history
Frames your stages, thoughts, identity
Ever as you pluck words from above
This scrivening room, this city,
House, sky or enfolding cave

# When I Die

When I die
You can identify my body
By a thumbnail

Once wounded
From some
Shrouded accident

Foggily remembered
As a metal door closing

With my baby teeth marks
Still remaining

With family mysteries
Still sealed

And unhealed

## Shatterlands

Where will we go, what will we do
When we forget what to renew

In the shatterlands of this new stage
Pondering shutters of another age

## How Did That Happen?

My medicines multiply
Like cats
Roaming the counters

I forget some of their names
Or why they have arrived

As long as services aren't called
To carry them out

# Fatigue

Books like old pets can't play with me
Magazines' perky to-do lists don't sing so brightly
My own advice tally seems smirky and cynical
Every corner of the house sighs
You didn't spend enough time with me

## Time Conundrum

When I have many empty hours, I'm petrified
I see a lone and snowy landscape before me
Filled with mines of criticism and contempt
So that my plans and actions seem futile

Though those are the very longed for spaces
That I thought would give me opportunities
For  clever organization, luminous projects
If only time could become my trusted friend

# Looking For

Looking for my badge
Getting nervously invested in the quest
Paying with limited time

Looking for my memory
Cells always being lost
Not a good sign

Looking for yesterday's day
Who knows where it existed
Or if things were ever perfectly fine

I realize now why that biblical lady
Partied after finding her lost coin
Life regained a happy rhyme

So may we all carefully, gratefully
Cherish cells, treasures, days and brethren
With heart, soul and caring mind

## Nostalgia, Solestalgia

Nostalgia – looking back
With rose colored glasses
To what maybe was

Solestalgia – an irrational
Homesickness for a virtual
Past that never was

Nostalgia for the people, places, things
That once mentored, nurtured me

Solestalgia for my never yet written
Or gathered history

## Healthy Goals

Doubt doubt!
Procrastinate procrastination!
Know what you don't know!

Invigorating signs
At the gym
To exercise your hand
As you scratch your head

And wonder
How to understand
And accomplish
Those confusing exhortations

## Once Advised

Feed the cherished pet goat
Make sweet lemonade out of sour fruits
Don't fear the other side of the moon
Get out of tradition's warm boxes
Tread on water trustfully

And those oceanic clouds
Those heavy grey vapors of worry
Turn to silver
Orange and gold

Harboring distant helicopters
Of good will

## Third Age Meditation

Parents, teachers, village dear
Where were you in our growing years?
What did you teach us so painstakingly
That we now think was always our identity?

Don't you deserve some later recognition
Even if mentor-fading is part of education
Let us therefore acknowledge your good works
And share your echoing, encouraging words

## Real or Fake

The foaming, the waves on childhood's shores
Is that my real souvenir kept forevermore
Or is it a fake memory from fancied stores

Picturing soapy bubbles teasing the sands
Recalling what adults reaching for my hand
In France's sunny, rescuing land

So many details the years have hidden
How then, exactly, when needed and bidden
Do complete autobiographies ever get written?

## Illness, Loss

New normal
Of illness, loss
Please
May it not happen
May it not stay

Yet, to cope
For our part
Let it not displace
Prayers and hope

In our thoughts
In our hearts

For renewed
Habits, health, energies,
Communications, commissions,
Charity and society

## Best Intentions

I wanted to give you wise advice
But I forgot what I was going to say
What kind of a mother could I be
With my haphazard ways
And neglectful old age

# In Our Day

– We did it better
In our day, in our way
Let us tell you about our methods
Listen as we have our say

Before we're driven into the sunset
Leaving this dream of a life
We have coped with so much
Let us share some of our lights

– Parents dear, older mentors
Let us have our say, do things our way
Surely we can follow our own roads
And we'll do so, come what may

– Beloved children, younger friends
Stay and hear our experience
We'll ask to help you always
And respectful prayers send

# Nurture

Sending you out
Beyond our home

With all the advice, mentoring, trajectories,
Expectations, graces, inspirations,
Support, priorities, vocabulary,
Cooking, tradition and taboos,
Chafings, resentments,
Interests and discouragements,
Hurts, resolutions,
Healings, feelings

I gave you

To cope and thrive
To make a better world

# Forgive Me

O Freda,
How have I treated you
When you could still hear me
Though not speak any more
Discussing your war years'
Incomplete stories

It was neither the time
Nor the place

Will you ever forgive me?
Will I ever forgive myself?

## Reasons and Excuses

Reasons require understanding
But excuses need to evaporate
With prayers of penitence
Lit by the Son of forgiveness
Rays of redemption

## More Needed For Whom?

Forgiveness, charity
Is it needed rather
For you or
For me?

## Twenty-Three and Everybody

Inside
Our DNA
With our personalities
We are, everyone
On varied places
On many different spectrums

Handling all twenty-three
More or less happily
All at once

# Time-Machined

Time-machined
By a typo mistake
What was I doing?
How old was I feeling
In twenty-zero-eight?

## Avatars

You may see me
As tactless, silly, selfish
Bitter, envious
Awkward, incapable
Or worse

But those are my avatars
Wrong spirits hovering
Not my inner soul

That yearns to be
Sophisticated, intelligent
Normal, helpful and good
Forgiven and understood

# Don't Judge

Don't judge my judgementalism
Don't criticize my criticism
Don't argue with my arguments
Don't frown at my witticism

Just empathize
Sympathize, contextualize
And, redemptively,
Harmonize

# Listen, Mind

Difficult it is
To readjust

Pavlovian dogs
Are the palate, taste buds
The growling stomach
Who beg for food
When possibilities are near

So listen, mind
Live life more carefully
Especially at your age

Say no to the mistaken voices
The set-points mourning the lost pounds
The beckoning calories
The grehlins of tiredness
The adrenalin of stress
The persuasion of conviviality
The false medals
When minute goals are reached

Be judicious
Live life wisely
With whatever's left
Dont eat frivolously

# Impressions Revised

Surprized, I found out
That inside
You have sore trials
Many burdens to carry
Problems unfair
A heavy cross to bear

Though when met
In gatherings
From the outside
It seemed first to me
That you hadn't a care
And radiated a perfect life
To emulate and share

Impressions revised
We could all use some help
Caring deeds and prayers

# Wings

They are winging it
Just as we all are
Like birds trying to fly far

## Just Wondering

Nineties wonder
If a hundred
Is a good goal

Eighties plow ahead slowly
Preparing for the nineties

Seventies want eighties
To be encouraged

Sixties wonder why seventies
Can't keep going steadily

Don't even ask about the fifties
Working on multiple ministries

When were we there?
What did we do?
How did we manage?

Lord, how little we knew

## Your Body Knows

Your body knows
How old you are

And so does the gravity
Of this marooned planet

Circling a milky way star
Not too close and not too far
From the sun's fearsome fire

Building your life's trajectory
Within earth's noisy bazaar

# Who Are You?

Identity –
Sense of purpose
Development trajectory
Comforting schedule
Definite work, habits
Authorized commissions, roles
Singleness of personality,
Fulfilling place in society
Accepted persona
Perception, conversations
Responses well-defined
According to revered traditions
All continued as taught

Although –
What about advice
To get out of the box
Develop new brain cells
Tour other languages, lands, plants
Meet more people,
Read mind-expanding articles, books
Collect knowledge, information skills
Change perspectives
Follow dreamed of hobbies

And retire
From that now
Tiring job

## Teachable Moments

Every moment teaches something
Everyone explains a little more
Thread by thread, drop by drop
Line by line

As we wander on winding paths
In puzzling woods
Wondering where or how or when
We'll be waiting
On the cloudy Jordan shore

## Evolving Zen Masters

We oldies
Are made Zen-aware
Of yet another

Complaining part of our bodies
Every aging day

And still later
Each sadly surprized hour

However
Let's not
Forget to thank God

For and with
What's left

## Aging Staircase

Aging staircase
Steps descending

Adjustments to be made

I thought I was very near
To the final landing

Yet here's another to tread

Carefully,
Thankfully

# The Supposed Healer

I knock on your door
A bit precariously I step in
Both somewhat wary of the other
You take the risk
Opening your heart to my own
Inviting me into the most sacred places
Of this last, most important journey.
I am honored by the invitation.
I, the supposed healer,
Offer what little I have:
A comforting word, a listening ear,
My simple presence in the chair
Sitting quietly as you breathe your last breaths.
My hand now rests upon yours
My fear replaced with love
For you, my dear one,
My fellow traveller
Your journey now leads you
Beyond where I can go
Leaving me to release you
To travel where I cannot
And I am left behind
To treasure the gift of life
You so freely shared
As I, the supposed healer,
Am healed.


--- Lisa Kearney

## Insomnia

Ideas careening around my head
Less like race cars, more as surfboards
On night oceans

## Voiced Insomnia

The network God gave you
Of time and space
Can be decorated with
Whimsical flowers of grace

Though your grid seem stricter
Than others' – leaving you
With strange sensitivities –
Less food choice

Yet aren't you glad insomnia
Gives you a writing voice

## Dream Diaries

Antennae of dreams
What do you pick up
And why

Diverse definite characters
I have never really met

Buildings intriguing
With various architectural styles
Exotic towns
I have never before visited

Strange landscapes, citiscapes
To figure out
To find my way around
Back home

Some quandaries unsettled
Some resolved with magic realism
Others by waking up
Into this dream life

## Room at Dawn

Light through the louvered blinds
Slowly spreads a filmy
Baby-blue cover
Over the bed and couch
Floors and walls
Of the awakening, stretching air
In the still sleep-laden room

## I'm So Grateful

I'm so grateful
My love and I
Are still in
This interactive house
Together

## While I Wasn't Looking

The dawn woke up, stretched,
Peeked through the window blinds
With its light blue greeting
While I wasn't looking –
Busily praying

## Dancing in the Light

Motes in the sunbeam
At a certain angle
Do you have a particular reason
For dancing down so graciously

## Hidden Possibilities

Multifaceted treasures
Hidden possibilities
The window seat can be a couch
The guest bedroom a study

Back bedroom half of a library
Back closet a manuscript depository
Fireplace niche can hold wood
Or an old doll house
That keeps many more stories

## Enough Room

To be so called
A room must have
Four walls, or is it five
Or maybe it's an oval

A room must have
A door or two
Unless it's a cave
Or inside an Irish tower

A room could have windows
Or maybe not
Decorations, a table, some chairs

Let there be secure, warm lights
Where good stories are told
For our souls to come in from the cold

# A Cinderella House

A Cinderella house
We once nabbed, now live in
Still keeps ashes in the fireplaces
From who knows when
Needy walls, baseboards
Dimmed windows

What would it take
To redress it, embellish it
With a makeover
For a spin
Of invitations

What would it take
Money, time and energy-wise
To make us
Fall in love with it
Again

## Cleaning by Tenses

As I try
To clean, organize
The house, closets
Endless papers
I wonder what I should
Throw out, downsize
To make place
For the limited present

Which meets and judges
Past plans, memories
And barks – no room, no room

Then the past pouts
And points out
Their great importance before –
Shouldn't previous
Cherished landmarks
Last forever?

They encircled
Your life, your world
How can you give
Those identifiers away

Dumping them
Intransigently
Into the river of time
Flowing ever faster

# Certain Chores

Certain house chores beckoning, bidden
Are like perennial weeds
Too often carelessly
Stepped over

While other projects and plans glow
Like decorative cultivated flowers
In your dreamy garden of goals

Let's live lovingly every moment
Cherishing those humble weeds also
How wisely deep-rooted
How surprizingly green

Some even waiting to be
Medicinal, restorative

# My Friend, This House

My friend, this house
I should think of your care

Not as a spiral, a whirlpool
Nor even as a road

But rather as a poem, a song
With regular, habitual refrains

Of inspired psalms
To hum as you're tended to

All day, week, month,
And, prayerfully, for
Many, many years

# Inside as Outside

Time, space, energy
What do you say
To the relativity

Of ironing the cloth expanse
Of a blouse, a shirt,
Shorts, trousers or skirt

With the iron as a spaceship
Seeking out all corners
Of its fibrous universe

## Who Loves Ironing?

God loves ironing
It's called redemption

Prepping, washing
Cleaning, drying
Removing dust particles

From the garments
Of our characters
Getting our souls ready
To celebrate in heaven

With Him

## To a Yellow Plaid Shirt

The yellow background evokes sunny skies
The dark blue lines fence in the hours
The narrower light blue lines not so evident
Limit the range of minutes lent

Plaid this life's structure
Patterned every language's
Take on existence

Showing how to express
With diverse creative designs
Gratefulness

## *Petite Fleur*

Do the next thing
As Elizabeth Elliot
Helpfully advised

Happily, graciously
As the Little Flower nun
Did with a song
Long, long ago

## Find Your Thanks

A calming balm to iron
Beautiful patterns
And colors hypnotizing

A blessing to empty the dryer
And warm your arms
With clouds of towels

A benefice to look around
As you clean, declutter
And see what can be found

A flavorful favor
To prepare and share meals
For health and pleasure

And the day isn't over yet

# Out of Date

The clothes in the less used closet, in boxes
Seem sad, yearning for a wearing
Appear to be humming
The Beatles' *Yesterday* song

Reminding – It's been too long
Now we're not only
Out of season
But out of date
Wasting away

Did you ever appreciate
Our careful tailoring
Our prints and decorations
More or less in fashion
Back in the day

## Downsizing Pains

Finally, at this time
Lacking space
I am actually
Thinking of
Donating, selling
Your winter coats
You made so well
I never needed

Six years after you died
A decade after you had to
Delegate your busy
Professional grade
Sewing machine

Death, that sadistic bully
Threatens at ever step
To make loved ones, their rainments
Lodging and legacies
Disappear

Does heaven have clothes closets
Within its sky mansions

To keep our rejected, dejected objects
That were our personal reminders
Of people, events, graces

That couldn't quite hop over
To bless next generations

# Typewriter Stroke

My dear typewriter
That I used so blithely
Not considerate of its hidden efforts
Sadly suffered a stroke

And now must be healed, helped
With more careful mindfulness
To write as fluently
As before

## Musical – Then and Now

Albums with
Needle-sensitive
Vynil tracks
Packed inside

How beautiful, musical
Shareable, tangible, visual
You were
In days of yore

Why did we leave you
When and where

For individual ear-buds
Or head-phones

For solitary, insular
Listening

Making yourself
At home everywhere

Alone

# *Outside*

# Morning Present

This bright morning I was
Kissed by a thin cobweb
As I got the newspaper

# The Street Hums

The street hums
With visible activities

One neighbor is getting a car sold
… There it went

Two houses are hosting service vans
Lawns being watered, roofs fixed
Garage sale advertised

Our next-door middle school
Buzzes with education
While an ice-cream truck waits
To sell students' learning rewards

Preteens now skateboarding, playing
Walking in two's and three's
Back home

Hopefully discussing
Their lessons, new knowledge
Preparing them for futures

Somewhere else

## Sun Commission

Sun, you have
Half an hour
To get up
To start washing
The sky in dawn blue
To start
The day's journey anew
To tell us
What God, our Creator
Wants us to do

## Bee Efficient

A neighboring lawnmower
Drones like an efficient bee
Outside my window

Warning that my cluttered thoughts
Have created weedy fields
Dusty surfaces, haphazard timing
And encouraged ADD butterflies

Maybe interesting
But useless if lazy
And disorganized

## It's Time

A pigeon cooed
With low note concern
Just outside the house

When an ancient, rickety
Bookshelf that had served
So faithfully in almost all
My years of teaching

Had to be carted out
Of the shamefully packed garage
Into the unbelieving sunlight

A sad foreshadowing
Of feared unravelling

# Taffy Time

Sweet leisure
Taffy time today
Stretching slowly
To infinity

## Eventide

I love those
Quiet late afternoon shadows
That linger pensively on lawns
And make long right-angle triangles
On lonely pavements and muse
About evening's soon
Deepening blue
Twilight

# Great Room at the Southwestern School of Art

Why, oh why did they redecorate?
Where are those wonderful colors of yesteryear?

The lime greens especially
Verdant, artistic, joyful

Recalled now only
By a green Wal-Mart bag
Abandoned on a brown table

Now all pale yellow are the walls
Thankfully enlivened by
The previous couch pattern
Of still cool black and white design

Floor to ceiling
Windows gaze at
Cloister walks

Built for the original convent
With its leafy patio,
Flowers abuzz,
Solemn fountain

Ever pensive, evocative
Lovely

## Garden at Trinity University

Through an open door
In an ivy-covered
Outdoor red brick wall

Waiting, we look into
A restful garden
Meditational bench and fountain

Imagining a cool, reflective
Moment within

Outside we can feel
Summer's relentless heat
In the parking lot
And across the hilly, extensive,
Seriously tended campus

## On the Way to the MARC
## (Medical and Research Center)

A wheeled office chair sitting still
In a green field looking at trees
City center skyline in the distance
All alone greets the morning

Yellow wildflowers take their turn
After the bluebonnets' short term
Breathing the fresh sunlight
Together greet the morning

Newly planted young trees
That supplanted venerable, axed oaks
By constructions' inexplicable design
Wave innocently in the morning

# From the Heights

Through grey clouds
Small pigeons zoom down canyons of buildings
Or rest on the roof
Of the facing ten-story medical facility

Tiny toy cars
Move slowly on play streets
And gameboard highways
In the angled evening light

Why so unhurriedly, slowly
In this busy big city
That demands serious speed?
Is it a trick of perception
From the heights of our hospital room?

Does God see us thus
From beyond our stratosphere
Smiling above His creation?

## Get-Well Bouquet


Sunrise opens like a flower
Trusting its segueing colors
To sweeten the day

Sky line of dark blue buildings
Their sharply outlined step blocks
Unchanged by the clock

Water tower like a giant
Immobile jellyfish
Grips the grey ground

In a quick minute all night lights
Give up their pinpoints efforts
Overwhelmed by the sun

That now, pale yellow
Brightens one distant wall
And sparkles the edge of another

While the gradually distinct greens
Of middle distance trees
Complete this morning's
Changeable painting

And very generous
Get-well bouquet

# Transported to the Ultra-Sound Room

Hello, ultra-sound reader
Are you a robot or a machine
Or a sentient cyborg

With your gold and green
Blinking lights for eyes
Your continuous wheezing
And your informational
Face of a screen

With wheels for feet,
Greyish plastic cords for limbs

Give us some encouraging news
Won't you?

# Waiting for Results

Minutes on the other
Side of nervousness
Ride by on a slow bicycle
Of the waiting morning

# Unbooked Half-Room

Shuffling around
Trying not to stumble
In this unbooked
Cramped cabin of a
Rehab half-room

Where each much
Rearranged bag of supplies
On miniscule shelves
In temporary storage
Represents the fuller contents
Of a whole room
Back at home

While remaining
Healing space is lent
To get-well posters
Cards and flowers
Brought by
Dearly praying
Family, friends

# Hearing What?

What is it that I hear
When I'm in a silent room?

Is it my mind chattering
Is it my emotions discussing

Is it the day's hushed vibrations
Is it God's breath in the center

Of nature's whirlwinds
While noise tries to

Creep into the cloistered garden
Of solitude

## At the Dealership

Indoor cars
Purr smuggly
Snugly in the showroom

Outdoor cars
Shiver, waiting
In the cold, cold rain

## Good Listeners

So wonderful the hair salon
All upbeat with up-dos
Sympathy of good listeners
Laughing with us at life's ironies
Much less bitter
When reviewed that way

## Lessons for a Substitute

Learn from students
Joie de vivre, energy

Learn from teachers
Plans, organization

Learn from classes
Interesting information

Learn from the halls
To navigate

Learn from changing schedules
Flexibility, cooperation

Learn from the outside trees
To pray

# Temporary

Right now I'm seated, ready
In this clean frosty blue room
With silent windows
And blank computer screens

The air conditioning hums
Its encouragement for me, a sub

Until youth-wise students occupy
The waiting desks, hopefully quietly

## Before Retirement

After the dismissal bell
Or when scheduled work is done

Pleasant to rest
In this space, on this bench
Next to this school parking lot

To meditate on
These clouds, this building, this sky

For a while, breathing
In time with its imperceptible
Planetary revolution

Around the always
Industrious sun

## After Retirement

Not so much a question of pacing oneself
As needed when teaching, grading tests

More a matter of creating rhythm and rhyme
In this variable, choice-filled, retirement time

# Campus Life Restarted (Without Me)

For weeks the junior high campus
Had been cleaned, polished, prepared
Classrooms and lessons organized
Teachers talked to, energized
Families invited and celebrated

Now walking, bus riding, driven
Students cajoled and/or motivated
With hopes on sleeve the first day
That the new learning year be kind
That peers be true, fun friends
That teachers lead well, understand

And we, the neighbors, pray
This sunny, late summer morning
That trajectories and identities
Be nurtured , shaped and guided
In God's fulfilling, wonderful way

## Little Boy Cute

Little boy cute
Quickly pushes
Importantly maneuvers
With his chubby toddler legs
A playcart without fuel
Around the playground
Of his daycare school

## Sister Nature

No better
Older sister
Than awesome
Nature

Let's stay
On good terms
Forever

## Nature's Clothes

Mother earth, sister sky
Brother sun, cousin ocean
Where did you get
Those beautiful clothes
Always finding patterns new

He's taken stardust
Woven all with care
Just be careful
With those holy vestments
Don't destroy or tear

# Not Helping

Diamonds wrested from the tortured ground
Mined for value, but at what price
Love for the glitter of treasures found
Though wonders on and
Above ground should suffice

# Drought

As a good-will substitute for rain's
All-encompassing, nourishing provision
I water each segment of the yard for what must be
A frustrating span of twenty seconds

Though that can paint thirsty grasses
And weeds with a hint of green.
I tease the leaves of trees. I don't know
If they are dancing with joy and I wonder

What's the use, what's the use?
But invisible birds chirp
Don't give up yet

And long rays from the gold-lending sun
Stream from trees to pavement while
The softly breathing, slightly cooler air awakens
With staccato summer cricket songs

## Out in the Microscopic World

A forest dense and mysterious
Within the branches of an arbor vitae
Whispers – Come closer and you'll get lost
In my shadowy greenery

An ocean in one drop escaping
From the water-hose in the morning
Drowns microbes, displays tiny diamonds
Without quenching the ground

A whole lawn, unplanned, nature-gardened
In one square foot of the yard's dry grass
Sporting vari-shaped leaves of weeds, flowerets even,
Creating an abstract green, yellow and brown design

A complete house in one corner of a room
Structured, furnitured like no other
Invites impulsive pauses and work
On special projects, often deferred

A world of little worlds flies away
When one soul is taken from this world's stage
Changing many characters' trajectories
Rewriting the lines, recalibrating the age

# Honor the Presents

A diamond in the rough
Shouldn't be roughly treated

A baby in the womb
Shouldn't be dispatched

A refugee child shouldn't be separated
From his family or locked up

An asylum seeker without a country
Shouldn't be shoved away

A planet so wondrous
Shouldn't be destroyed

God become human to help us
Shouldn't be disrespected,
Scorned or despised

## Stop Objectifying

If good will and grace be joined
We can talk with the trees
We so mindlessly perceived

We can converse with the ocean
Hearing in its roars and murmurs
The saga of all creation

We can communicate with the animals
As they speak their sorrows
With their eyes

And we can stop our selfish
Objectifying

## Cattle Moved

Cattle in the rolling
Cattle car

Huge eyes questioning
Through slats

Looking around
Tightly bound
Not knowing
If towards death

Not making a sound

## No Matter How Pretty

Don't pick those flowers
No matter  how windblown, tiny
Purple, pretty, lacelike
Or curiously, mutantly pink
Among yellow weed blooms

Don't tear and don't doom them
They're already yours
As you noticed them
And rejoiced

# Can Anyone Hear?

Musically branched
Grove of oak trees

Does no one
Hear you sing
See your wavy dances
Know your work
To clean our skies

And sweep away
Our too triumphant
Predatory footprints?

Rosary of small red flowers
On green summer bushes
Does no one heed

Your calls to prayer for
Our families, neighbors?

## Wonderfully Framed

Blooming so beautifully
After down-bending rain

The punctually flowered
Sage bushes bend
Into a green and purple
Heart shape

Framing and embracing
Our turquoise fountain

# Fish, Boats and Butterflies

The swift, colorful fish
Darting in and out of home reefs
Are the butterflies of the deeps
Not for many human eyes to see

My thoughts swim in waters
Sadly becoming ever shallower
While younger boats in modern lanes
Enjoy sailing ever faster

Who will love the fish, boats and butterflies
What will be left of their moving adventures
Sea deep or sweet flower wise
Whisper of wings or swish of fins unheard

## Look Up

Clouds like cotton-candy continents
Mapped in the ocean-like blue sky

## Adorable, Vestigial

Dear vestigial dinosaur
Tiny bird flying high
Above the clouds

Do you mind looking so adorable
As you soar on your reptilian wings
And terror now to insects bring

## *Quo Vadis?* – Where Are You Going?

In the bemused, becalmed twilight
With its good-bye puffy peach clouds
Minute birds singly or in groups
Hastily fly

They seem to know
Exactly where or why

They need to forge
An unmarked roadway
In the storm-washed sky

# Leading, Led

Two dogs led with leashes
On the morning sidewalk
In tandem

Smiling broadly
So happy-proud
To walk their master

## Temporary Memorial

Sunflowers
Do you remember
The clouds and the rain
The heat and the cold?

With your friendly faces
You commemorate
And decorate
The condemned
Trailer park

With its roadside cemetery
For our beloved pets

Who looked up to us
As we look to
Our warming sun

# Watching

Black tiger cat prowls
In our over-tall green grass
Whiskers caressing the rain-grown blades

Cleans itself, rests
Green defiant eyes not minding
That I am watching

## Thin Strands

Thin amber strands of water
Dance in the backdrop of air

Grasses and weeds
Try to become green

They reflect the setting sun
Now even the bushes
Turn to gold

As the twilight minutes revolve
Rivulets turn silver

Then the street hushes
Angels spread their mauve blankets
Above the still parched ground

## Limestone Keepers

Grazing in fields of green
Great white limestone rocks
Rest in the distance
Like a company of pale cattle

Some also guard
Driveways, tended front yards
Marking boundaries
Singly or single file

Peculiar pride
Of this fair city —
The boulders stand
As lone sentinels
Or form
A sparse line-up
Of stalwart ghost soldiers

Maybe still, silently
Defending this town
With its mission churches
And historic fortress

Harking back
To the harrowing
Alamo test

## Code Switching

Cenizo / sage – a wise bilingual plant
Switching to a different code
Of purple blooms
Every once in a while

Presents mauve bushes
All around town, on the hills around
An intermittent, southwestern
Rain-celebrating song

## Baroque Painting in the Sky

Skies over the highway's busy stream
Grey clouds form a wavy frame
Around an echoing blank expanse of
Pinkish coral colour
That recedes to almost reveal
The heavenly home
Of baroque angels
Waiting to be seen

# I'll Get the Mail

So many things to notice
In the lesser rains

The braided stream
Of the gutter's running waters
Bubbles here and there
With clear joy

A soft grey
Curious pigeon
Steps gingerly
Across the street
On pink feet

While others coo
The storm is almost over

Come out and play
Fly with us for a while
In the calmed pale blue
San Antonio skies

# April Fool

First of April
Blooms with possibilities
Trips with probabilities

Laughs – Surprize!
You have perceived wrongly
The bars of time, the slide of space

As you tried to readjust
To daylight saving
And this greening season

April Fool! – I tricked you
I can get chilly still
It's not totally spring yet

## Flower Music

The bass notes of the deep purples
The baritones of the bluebonnets
The tenors of the Indian paintbrushes
The mezzo-sopranos of the pinkish mauves
The high sopranos of the yellow
And white flowers

Arranged on the hills, medians and lawns
Experimenting with harmonizing
Are really choirs visiting our paved cities
That joyfully present us with their
Sadly ephemeral gifts of song

They know that our souls
Thirst for their landscaping notes
Yet can't modernly live
With nature too much or too long

## Record Breaking Heat

Watered the many happy weeds
And the few melancholy grasses
For several seconds, each section
To prove my compassion

Heard the sarcastic cicadas
Clicking their cynical songs
Complete with answering stanzas
Enjoying summer's sun-heated saunas

Saw the satirizing sparse clouds
Pretending to hold some rain
Holding out ten percent possibilities
Devoid of real probabilities

## Atacama Desert Discovery

A travelogue documents
A miniscule colorful flower
Alone and lost in endless sand
And rocks

Follows
A lone botanist who sets out
To research this plant
For our needs

The voice-over asks
How in the dry world
Does it survive
Without visible water
For eighty years
Or more?

I hope the scientist
Doesn't pull it out
By its spreading roots
To investigate
Its secret

Killing the only plant
For miles around

The science documentary
Didn't say

# Future Explorers

The still steaming tar marks
Look like Nazca lines in the Atacama desert

Except these glisten black on broken pavement
Except here there are trees
Plants and hills all around

Except these lines are curved and wavy
One even looking like a backward question mark

Maybe future explorers from on high
Flying over this later, possibly deserted,
City outdoor mall

Will deduce messages, worship paths
In our haphazard linear art

## Still Summer

The rattle of enduring summer heat
As theme music played by crickets
Calling each other across the torpid street

A helicopter flies overhead
Its shrill whirls louder than any insect

A dried yellow root runner with
Tufts of grass turned to hay
Like a crown of thorns
Carelessly strewn on our struggling lawn

That acts as a dramatic touch
Brought by languid breezes
That move brown leaves humidly

This afternoon, fulfilling
The repetitious daily forecast

## Cloud Personalities

Some clouds balance
In the summer sky
Like solitary sloths
Then move slowly closer

To the sharks and the lambs
The angels and the cotton candy
The seahorses and fish
Whispy formations

But the southwestern sun
Chases all clouds away

Maybe they'll eventually
Win the weather war

And it will rain again
Some other blessed day

## Tell Me

Is this the foretold
Norther blowing into
Our fair city?

Tell me

O green hands clapping
Sago palm
Tell me

Our mysteriously
Ever growing pine
Tell me

Joyous cenizos
Purple dancing now
Tell me

Waving sheets of needles
Within the arbor vitae
Tell me

Wondrously tall mesquite
And shivering bushes

Tell us

And let us celebrate
The new autumn weather
With you

# Finally

Strong gusts suddenly
Sway rejoicing branches
Sending brown leaves
Scurying down the street

Rain tap-dances
Rhythmically on the
Once-bored skylight
Washing dust-dry windows

Thunder mutters distant comments
From heavy-browed clouds

That chastise and chase away
Our months-long drought

## The Character of Water

Water…soft, clear, never grating
Falling in delicate drops

Torentially moves
Massively immobile boulders
And plucks up trees
As just so many potted plants

For thundering speeches
About climate changes

## Sleepless in the Sky

The clouds can't sleep either
Tossing and turning in their sky-bed

Their lightning nightmares
Darkening our rooms and streets

## Oak Tree's Concern

Just wanted to make sure
You got exactly
The same number of acorns
On your driveway

That you swept away
With so much effort
Just a few hours
Ago

## Moon Moods

Silver moon above dance halls
Golden moon over harvest hills
Blood moon crying its warnings
Blue moon that we don't heed

For, we haven't hesitated
To walk on its dusty grey surface
Leaving our newsworthy footprints
And landing debris

## Moth or Butterfly?

Folding and opening
A tiny fan clings
On our winter grass
Cunning pattern, brown and yellow
… Is it a moth or a butterfly?

If a moth, it's my closet's warning
Of tigers hiding in sheep's clothes
If a butterfly, it summarizes
Surprizing beauty, delicate hopes

## Snow in San Antonio

Our arbor vitae trees
Are Christmas costumed
Like northern pine trees
With their branches weighed down
By pillows of snow

Is this a beautiful promise
A surprizing New Year's gift
And Chanukah sign
That seasons will return
To our peace-imagining earth

## Sacrifice

The trees, the prayerful trees
Always bear presents for us

Oxygen exchange
For our carbon dioxide
Lovely canopies
Protection from wind and rain
Coolness from too much
Of our scrutinizing sun

Moreover one type
Dubbed Christmas
Is killed, sacrificed
For many

To donate for our holiday
Gifts, lights
And at the summit
A reminding
Guiding star of love

# Don't Give Up

Poor painted clown-face flowers
Shivering in the unseasonal wind
Take heart
We're in San Antonio
Soon to warm

## Winter to Spring

Do you remember
The winter grasses wore
Yellow and beige rags
Waiting
To be kissed by cloud princes

Now they awaken
With green yawns

Giving their old, dry clothes
To small papery butterflies

Showing off
Dancing south

# Resting by the Side of I-10 to Brownsville

Will there be drama in the painted landscape?
Will the clouds move into new configurations?
Will birds land on scraggly mesquite branches?
Will the furry beige grasses wave expectantly?

Waiting for our eyes to caress them lovingly
Waiting for our wheeled abode to resume rolling
Waiting to rejoin the clear zooming highway
Waiting for the rest of the journey
To our previous home

## Driving Back from Brownsville

The tall grasses by the highway
Comb their yellow hair in the wind
The cars and trucks
Hum high, impatient notes
The signs on the side
Race to somewhere in
The opposite direction
Field furrows planted with some crop
Quickly form more acute angles

A train on a parallel track
Rests disconsolately
Multi-colored wild flowers splash
Abstract-patterned carpets
On the road's median and shoulders

Low dark clouds
Above the land
Threaten and promise
Soon rains for
Farms and ranches

Easy listening music
Goes in and out of range

The still flat horizon
Starts to undulate
And hints about

The soon end of the trip
Back to our present

Home

# We're Ready

Weeds, vines and
Bushes like small trees
Overhang the highway walls

Murmur – We're here
Ready to cover
This land, this earth when
Your anthropocentric era
Is over

## Mercado, San Antonio

Celebrate!

Purple, yellow, red confetti
Decorate the pearl-gray
Second level parking pavement
Otherwise well regimented

But we can walk down to
The fiesta sounds, sights and smells
Of the Mercado

Though we could ask
Which one will win in the end?

Will we eventually
Have a completely paved planet
Bland, uncompromising structures

Or will the music, colors, cooking
Culture's celebrations
Live and win
As do grasses
Through cement

Though global warming
Our careless footprints
May eventually
Desiccate all
Anyway

# Walk in Schnabel Park

We needed to get out
Of the sadness that haunts
Our long ago histories

Into the healing quiet
Of green trails
Perfumed by peeling cedars
Greeted by bandana-decorated dogs
Grinning proudly

A serious deer
Still as a statue
Contemplated us

At the end of the trail
Peppy children warned

Not to keep going
Past the edge of the cliff

By a memorial to a girl
Who did

# After Movie – *One Year in Siberia*

What is freedom?
Asked the movie
About the endless expanses
Of the Siberian *taiga*

Its snowy wilderness
Promising liberation
From noisy, levelling pavements
Of a materialistic society
That doesn't allow for
Or develop a deep interior
Individualistic identity

Or is it freedom to choose to battle
With a nature cruelly cold and bleak
Though often beautiful, exhilarating
With its icy skies, graceful birches
And pines on dark hills sloping under
A full white lamp of a moon

## After E.M. Forster

A question opens up
A mind conversation
To infinity

Be ready
Then you can
See the path
To a good answer

Responding
Sensitively
Positively

And listening
To the silences
As well

# Where Do They Come From?

Positive words:
Constructive values,
Hope, life, goodness,
Beauty, peace, happiness,
Freedom, love, kindness

All come from Thee, God

For what do we have
Inside ourselves
In our societies

What resides in our thoughts,
DNA reactions
In our speech:

So many negatives
That make Thee cry

### *D'où Viennent-Ils?*

*Les mots positifs:*
*Les valeurs constructives*
*L'espoir, la vie, la bonté,*
*La beauté, la paix, le bonheur*
*Liberté, amour, gentillesse*

*Tous ceux-là viennent de Vous, Seigneur*

*Car, qu'avons nous
Dans nous-mêmes
Dans nos societés*

*Qu'est-ce qui habitent
Dans nos pensées
Dans nos réactions d'ADN
Dans nos discours:*

*Tant de négatifs
Qui Vous font pleurer*

# Word Game Prizes

To communicate oral messages
To play the word game
Ever anew

Speaker and hearer
Must know what phonemes
Or combinations thereof
And pitch, intonations

Are undisputably
Meaning-sending morphemes

Prizes that God
Wanted us to have
And use
Amicably

# Bitter Flowers

Bitter flowers
Hurting words
In your mind
Saddening your heart

Throw them away
Another day
God will give you
A sweeter bouquet

*Beyond*

# Words Once Acquired

Words once acquired
Scaffolded
By solid grammar

Can discern concerns
In mansions of interests,
Apartments of reactions,
Rooms of feelings
Within

And outside
Provide infinite
Windows to observe
Clouds, trees and sun
Nature and passers-by

Then, more inspiring
Than silent dreams,
Loving words
Let us scan
Skies beyond

# To Write On

Paper, papyrus, hides and stone
To lead our memories to needed homes

Stone, hides, papyrus, paper
So that our lives won't vanish as vapors

# After Emily Dickinson – *To Make a Prairie*

To make a class
It takes one student
A teacher
And lessons plans
Not a few

And a room

Or, if that isn't present
Any welcoming space

With windows
To a happy beyond

Will do

# Library Analogy

Somewhere in my childhood
I would be left, after school
By my work-seeking
Immigrant family

In a community library
Next to an elder home
Finding myself in its antique room
With heavy wood furniture

Full of wondrous books
Of woven mysteries
Fairy-tale collections
Sparkling stories
Hiding sage life lessons

Now at the other end
Of my span's spectrum

I heard on public radio
A beautiful analogy
Of Creation
As a huge library

Full of wise books
With endless explanations

Some in foreign languages
That our childlike minds
Can't completely decipher
Yet

## Books Ubiquitous

Books in shelves, on tables
In the libraries
In the mansions
Of the great beyond

Where opened pages
Are turned to answers
To earthlings' questions
About redemption

And the windows
Glow with rays bright
Of truth and beauty
With God's loving light

## Book Club with C.S. Lewis, Martin Buber

Two books by my bedside
Close to each other

Are you discussing philosophically
Your varying viewpoints of God

In nature, in providence, in miracles
In relation with each creation

Offering points to ponder
Disagreeing pleasantly

In your inaudible, printed
Constant, important

Conversation

## After *Plato and a Platypus Walk Into a Bar* – by
## T.W.Cathcart and D.M. Klein

Plato and a platypus shuffled into a bar
  – How curious, said Plato, I don't know if you are
A shadow or a real idea from the divine Lord
  – Yes, I exist, as you do, according to His word

Then let's together write, sing and philosophize
About God who has given us many a cool surprize
Let's toast His goodness, chill, and talk about
His creation, inspiration with Plato and the platypus

## Caves – After Plato's allegory in ***The Republic***

Caves so comfortable
Give us known shadows
Of half- truths

Outside too bright
To quickly recalibrate
The surprizing sunlight

Of God's numinous kingdom

# After *Gravity and Grace* by Simone Weil

Dear Simone Weil
While you were writing purely
Of purity, did you love those insights,
Realize that they would be scattered widely
To perplex and make people ponder

The sufferings and hurts so continous
The hopes of Christianity so veiled
Intermittently twinkling
As the highest star
In the deepest sky

# After *Brontë* by Glynn Hughes

The Brontes, such brave short-lived
Canaries in the coal mines
Near newly industrialized towns

The family chased by ash-laden tuberculosis
Trying to cry their gothic-romantic songs

Living a dark  prefiguring
Of all our perishing
Due to our selfish carbonizing
This once viable planet

# After NPR Interview with Michael Collins – Astronaut

Behold this globe
Tiny, beautiful
Blue and rust
Marbled with oceans, clouds
And mountains like dunes

Our earth wants, it cries
To be looked at, to be treasured
As it circles the sun
And dances in time with the moon

# Precursor

Her face
Mysterious and satisfied

Multiple copies of
Mona Lisa's smile
Are often enlisted

To persuade us on various ads
How wondrous and cool
Our modern products can be

Was Leonardo da Vinci a precursor
Of the advertising industry too?

## Notre Dame, Paris, April 15, 2019

Having inspired breathtaking art
And saved it for eight hundred years

When its complex beauty of patterns
Crashed into our form-breaking, careless fires

Where were you, Our Lady of Paris?

## Guatemala Travelogue

The colors you see
On this bright scarf,
That patterned blanket

Came from our fruits,
Flowers, grasses and leaves

I gathered to dye
Spin and weave

This and more
I learned from
My eco-friendly ancestors
To teach my family, village
And curious tourists

About our mutual world

# Forever a Road Trip

A book is always a road trip
Taking you out of
Your well-known rooms
With other people driving you
Through new landscapes

A visit is definitely a road trip
Expanding hearth and heart
As objects are moved to new locations
Wisdom and histories reviewed
Conversation and entertainment shared

A dream is a sometimes
Remembered road trip
Kaleidescoping crazily
Bits of waking journeys
Realistic quandaries
Combined with
Peculiar, unknown places

# The Kaleidescope Cure

Beyond the day's formalities
Bits of colored cardboard cues
In a medley of forms array nightly
In quick-moving patterns

Then accumulate as rambling stories
Their surprizes continuously unfolding
Their narratives never quite finished
Their plots dropped but still echoing

With the relief
Of awakening

## Soular Universe

Passing through
The clock face
The calendar quilt
Also

To a place
Beyond veiled memory
Or familiar topography
Or habitual choreography

To a new
Soular universe
Dancing to
Otherworldly
Music

## Dreams to Poems

In sleep forests
Dreams go collecting
Wild flowers of the day

That waking poetry
Can arrange tomorrow
Into musical bouquets

# One Difference Makes a Difference

One difference
Between metaphor and illusion
Symbol and hallucination

May be

Whispy lines of likeness
Growing too strong

# Poems to Prayer

Sometimes it's a lilting line
Sometimes a group of grumbling words
Sometimes it's an observation shared
Maybe a commentary on a natural
Or man-made curiosity

Sometimes it's a quandary
That won't let go
Until it's transformed
Into a prayer

# Poet Tree Island

Marooned in a library room
Our Poet Tree island
Has one maroon wall
Punctuated with grand
Park-glimpsing windows

The rest of the room yellow
With a moon-map poster
To give a telescopic view

As we discuss life,
The universe anew

# Possibilities

Story-telling or descriptive writing
Philosophizing versus detailing
Portraying people, nature, artifacts
Analyzing histories, feelings
One thing or another

So many poetic possibilities
No two are alike
As snow flakes they drift
From the skies of our poetry sessions
And delight our imaginations

Changing some worryscapes
Into wonderlands bright

## Poetry Assembly Line

A pencil to start
A pen to rewrite

A clear plastic holder
Next to the typewriter

For easy reading
Fun revising

A computer Word program
To file and reorganize
To categorize and formalize
After playing around often
With words and lines

All to be arranged
In tangible ringbinders
Then in virtual files

This assembly line
For written meditations
This personal industrial revolution
A miracle, considering
My messy, cluttering habits

## You Are My Favorite Poem

You are the song
The poem, the grace
My sunshining love
In every stage and place
Of our years together

You are many poems and songs
Historical, philosophical, romantic
Companiable traveller
Co-student and teacher

Spelled with wonder, rhymed with generosity
Reflecting God, Savior and Holy Spirit

# Once Told

That I shouldn't waste time reading
Or thinking about university
That those doors would be locked
That I shouldn't even try

But I asked around, begged around
And suddenly I could, did attend
Those lectures partly in that
Wonderful musty auditorium that
Had first enchanted me
Discussing literature classics quite openly
That I had read on the sly

Then, the next year, same place
I met up with, studied with
My soul mate, *bashert* for life
A match made on high

## *Bashert* – Arranged in Heaven

When
You were a little boy
Roaming in the woods

I was
A little girl
Looking for you
Looking for me

You had a church, a farm, a forest
Kansas City, New York, Houston, Austin
I had forgotten Poland
Well-loved Paris, then fine Montreal
With its Mount Royal
Trails for two

And finally
We were both in the same place
At the same time

Surprized to recognize
The search was over

## Out of the Clear Blue Sky

Not yet touching
We walked in the snow
On clouds
In the winter city
That sang
And caressed us
Prophetically

Love
Out of the clear blue sky
Of your eyes

Enveloped us,
Set us free
To be happy

Together
Whatever
The weather

## In the Kingdom of Love

The heart
With its curvilinear
Triangular shape
Like the silhouettes
Of two fetuses
Facing each other
One the child
And one the mother

The heart
Two rainbows
Elliptical
Delineating paths
Spiritual

The heart
Two shadows
Turning a corner
The meeting of
Two surprized loners

Who become
Changed beings

In the kingdom
Of love

## Not Even Half-Begun

Clouded identities
Half-begun, labyrinthian
Convoluted stories
On the shadowed, scattered
Pages of our lives

Only God can turn
And find a pressed flower
Of a soul poem inside

That survives
To be fully revived
In His eternal
Garden kingdom

## As One

Take your shoes off
Those soles of your soul
That touch the sad, messy ground
Carelessly, pragmatically
Following causality

Meditate on what astounds
Walk into numinous visions

And you and God will discuss
That what was lost spiritually
Can be found

And you will wonder
As one

# Towards the End

Remember the love, the family, the people
Who have ministered
In your life

Know the poetry
The rhymes, the metaphors, the music
Within your life

Count the molecules
The atoms, the strands
Throughout your life

Figure the formulas, the charts
The projects, plans, schedules, roles
For your life

Perceive the opportunities,
The miracles, the rescuers
Of your life

Meet and greet God
Who creates, leads, comforts
From above your life

## Photos with Radio

Radio music with
Mournful violin strings
Tie together into
A melodious present
For afternoon contemplation

Those years-ago family photos
On top of our bookshelves
Offering an endless
Memory circle
Of love

## We Are All Walking Wounded


We are all bag people
Dragging our rags
And tatters ever so carefully

Through this unpredictable
Forest of a life
With traps and pitfalls rife

Grasping at bits of dreams,
Paper plans,
Discarded hats,
Fleeting funds
And ephemeral fun

We are all walking
Wounded in the foggy
Morning light among
Taupe trees praying
Grey clouds writing
On the blue
Parchment of the sky

Yet somewhere
In a parallel universe
Beyond our lands
Of illness and worries
Time and money

Abides a kindly kingdom
Bright and lovely

Where truth and wisdom
Comfort and walk
With all travellers
Towards their homeland spiritual

# Sermon at St. Francis

The Holy Spirit as the whispering wind
That moves where it wills
That carries like far-travelling feathers
The leaves of the wonderful word

That alight first on one place
Then another
Persuading one person
Then the next

Healing, restoring
With their tender touch

## I Corinthins:13 – Beyond

Beyond the ugly tips of danger
Above the mud of terrible news
Through clouds of worrisome trends

Shines the Son of love
His redeeming rays
Warming our hearts and souls
Abiding over all

www.ingramcontent.com/pod-product-compliance
Lightning Source LLC
Chambersburg PA
CBHW051755040426
42446CB00007B/370